Places That Are Gone

Karen Friedland

Nixes Mate Books
Allston, Massachusetts

Copyright © 2019 Karen Friedland

Book design by d'Entremont
Cover photograph from the collection of Lauren Leja

All rights reserved. This book or any portion thereof may not be reproduced or used in any manner whatsoever without the express written permission of the publisher except for the use of brief quotations in a book review or scholarly journal.

ISBN 978-1-949279-15-3

Nixes Mate Books
POBox 1179
Allston, MA 02134
nixesmate.pub/books

*For Rich, the Poetry Sisters,
and all of my beloved friends*

Contents

Part I

Blue Blanket	2
Springing	3
Kind Women	5
A Revelation	6
Oh God, What Were Their Names?	7
Scotch	9
The Peach	10

Part II

The Wizard	12
An American Girl	13
Bait Dogs	14
Ahimsa	16
Babies in Jam Jars	17
High Heels	18
Gone	19
Elderberry Wine	20
Spring Rain	21

Part III

Pound	23
Emptying Last Year's Pots for This Year's Flowers	24
Sugars	25
Tattered Curtains	26
Today, by God	27
Only Connect	28
Nothing	29
Everything	30
Green Gift	31

Part IV

Half a Century In	33
Lost Thoughts	34
Summer Library	35
Dust Bowl on TV	36
I Can See Why Sylvia Plath Killed Herself	38
A Prayer for Rough Sleepers	39
Kindred Spirits	40
Grateful for Parties	41
Making the Stew	42
These Limpid Days	44
Hosta Horns	45
For Layla	46

Places That Are Gone

Part I

Blue Blanket

I married you, yes,
but I miss your bachelor apartment –
the stale smell, the layer of dust,
the green treetops from your bedroom window,

the stitched-together blue blanket
I made you throw away –

your cats, their fur,
the early '90s
and the music we listened to
back then.

Springing

There's a panic
to the coming flowers,
like slow, eagerly-anticipated fireworks –
Crocus! Oooh! Daffodil! Aaaah! Tulip!

To the trees, budding frantically,
and the roiling gray skies looming above us,
portending change by the minute,
just as we'd gotten accustomed to winter.

There's far too much tenderness
in early spring –

the fallen sparrow's egg,
its unhatched chick still inside;

the green leaves unfurling,
already chewed to lace by a nonindigenous caterpillar
working its way up the coast;

the pale green day lilies emerging,
only to be crushed by oafish, heavy work boots.

"Life's not fair, kid,"
as Dad would say.
"Life's not fair."

Kind Women

Kind women,
who live in cities,
and who love beauty

inevitably grow plants so big,
they could be trees,
reaching for the ceiling
as if reaching for the sky.

Kind women think nothing
of giving books, food and cuttings
to wanting younger women
who stop by –

books that line bookshelves over the years,
and cuttings that grow huge and leafy
and act as talismans do,

spreading their gnarled green grace
on passersby.

A Revelation

It's a revelation
how dusty
a house can get,

and how familiar you are by now
with every spider lurking in every corner
patiently waiting for the dusting to end
while the old, blind dog
barks for your attention.

Oh, your aching back and head,
as you clean inch by inch
towards wood-gleaming beauty

For all you ever really wanted
was a home.

Oh God, What Were Their Names?

The co-worker I cried in front of –
you know, that older guy at the shelter –
when I found out my kitten was going to die?
I hear he's dead now, too.

The gay guy, in drama class
we were all so sure was going to rule the world –
I look down at my toothpaste –
was his name Tom?
Where is he now?
in New York, failed,
like the rest of us?

That co-worker whose name
I could never, ever remember
for the life of me,
not when we chatted at work for over a year,
not when I saw her later on the street –
this sheer inability haunts my dreams.

My brain lacks space, it seems,
for all these names

though, yes – the now-dead man at the shelter –
his name was Al.
I remember that now.

Scotch

Even as a child,
I understood the deep kind of tired
that old folks got
that had them laying
fully-clothed
on sofas by late afternoon.

I'm middle-aged now,
and tired,
and the old folks are all gone
such as laid down in the afternoon with their shoes on,
loosened ties
and poured scotch over ice.

Except in our home,
where we keep these traditions alive.

The Peach

Bite into it!
commanded the old man,
offering me a peach
at the Georgia roadside stand,

and when I hesitated –
"Just bite into it!"

And when I did
and smiled,
he smiled and said
"Isn't she sweet?"

Part II

The Wizard

In her months of dwindling,
a kind man created a story for her –
about a young boy swept off a Kansas farm
to a magical land with little people
and a yellow brick road.

Like Scheherazade,
he kept the adventure going,
but so that she, not he,
might live another day.

And then, in the spring
she died anyways,
and in his grief,
the kind man wrote down his tales,
but made the hero a heroine instead,
to honor a little neighbor girl he'd loved
named Dorothy.

And so, in the end, he
saved many a girl.

An American Girl

The pale blue polyester pants
that old men wore up high in those days,
while they sprayed pesticide in every crack
and swept up every last leaf, impenetrable.

And the glee of the muddy, shouting girls
playing in the creek with sparklers,
back before they even knew
they had bodies.

And the tipped-ear,
smiling little reddish-brown dog,
who might live 14 or 15 years
if you're lucky,
and they don't give her away –
you'll remember her kind eyes, always.

Bait Dogs

Bait dogs
are usually female –
this one was left for dead
on a cold winter night
by Turtle Pond.

She had more than 60 bite wounds,
some hand-sewn with purple thread,
others still fresh, infected.

Sixty flashing sets of teeth
tore at this dog's flesh,
and yet she wagged her stump-tail
when her rescuers came.

She was harmless, helpless
and will need six months of quarantine
because they don't know how many dogs bit her.

All I can hold onto
is how grateful I am for her rescuers,
for the all-night animal hospital they raced her to

and even for the t.v. newswoman
who reported this story
that made me cry for days.

Ahimsa*

My Dad liked tripe,
pig's trotters, veal, calamari
and the like –
all manner of murdered species.

In our last night together,
at the hospital,
I kept the channel locked to "Weird Food,"
because I thought he'd like it,
then left the room
when the inevitable killings happened –
small rodents skewered,
furry, confused lambs being slaughtered,
a cow's head made into cheese.

You could say
it was a vegetarian's revenge,
but then I never saw him again,

so you could say
no one won that one.

*Sanskrit word meaning "non-violence toward all living things"

Babies in Jam Jars

It's an ark of sorts,
this old wooden house,
adrift on the sea of the world,

with two cats, two dogs, two humans –
only we're all fixed or middle-aged,
so there'll be no reproducing,

save for the myriad plants
which have multiplied
many times over –

my babies in jam jars
by the kitchen window
that I keep trying to give away.

High Heels

She stumbles along in high heels,
like a queen who wants to be taller than she really is,
in order to rule the sidewalks
and men's hearts –
to beat out all those other dames
in this hapless game of domination in the city.

When all she really wants is to curl up like a cat,
catching breezes through the gumwood windows,
ink smudged on her fingertips,
her little black dog poised
to defend her against anyone and everyone

Gone

is that long-shuttered, freaky, pansexual nightclub
we danced in, to '80s music –
Man Ray, it was called.

Gone is the old grove of green trees
glowing yellow with lichen
we walked through, my dog and I,
before it was shorn off and plowed under
and turned into houses.

Gone is the once-young, dancing body I had,
grown withered and bony, pot-bellied and pained,
although sometimes it dreams that it's young, still.

Elderberry Wine

Old, wrinkled sex organs
are never pretty,

but let's get it on, baby –
let's not even pretend we're young.

Let's be honest
for once,
about what gets us going,

and what prayer-like convocation
might actually
happen between us this time.

Spring Rain

is falling –
forget your silly, constant pain.
Unearth beds!
There are birds to be fed –

Tiny sparrows on branches
with cocked heads
are waiting for you
to step into the day.

Part III

Pound

Pound the earth
does my neighbor Linda Burke,
in her quest to subdue it –

she hacks back tree limbs,
disassembles moss
and plants tomatoes that fail
year after year after year.

And yet in spring,
Here she is, in the rain –
Pounding and pruning and hoping again.

Emptying Last Year's Pots for This Year's Flowers

The desperation of the roots –
having filled their tiny chambers to completion,
wanting so much more than this world could give them.

I load old pots with last year's soil
but remove the hungry roots
coiled in circles – the reminder

that we are all of us wanting,
reaching and desperate beyond measure
to keep on growing.

Sugars

Trees communicate,
it turns out –
they feed sugars
to the roots of their friends
for centuries
after they've been chopped down.

This makes me feel slightly better
about the murdered, giant beauties I mourn every day,
assuming they had friends other than me,
who can do nothing.

Tattered Curtains

That sweet, New England-starchy old man
in an ancient bathrobe
who always reached down and scratched
behind my old dog's ears,
who lived for years in that ramshackle green
ranch-house down the street

must have died, because they're taking down
all the big trees in his back yard,
and next the shrubs, and now the small house itself,
in just one day,
that bore the same frayed, plaid bachelor curtains
for years.

And another old soul has gone up in smoke
and drifts away, along with the souls
of the big, leafy green trees
that lived as if forever in his overgrown back yard.

Today, by God

everything is beautiful –
the early-turning leaves from the kitchen window
the neighbor's one-note wind chime
the dog's sigh.

I wonder
how people can ever do evil
when old wood in a house
glows amber this way.

Only Connect

Summertime teenagers
laugh raucously on street corners,

evening cicadas beat out a symphonic roar,

the sleeping kitten puts all four paws
on my bare leg –

she craves contact –
we all do.

Nothing

On a day this beautiful,
nothing should die –
not a possum on the road,
not a bee in clover.

Everything

Everything led to this –

A vigorous pot
of Black-Eyed Susans
that grew of their own accord.

Green Gift

There are times –
usually late afternoons
in late summertime –
when everything feels holy
and every teacup blessed.

When the train whistles low,
and the sun streams through dark green leaves,
and sets before you know it.

When dogs bark into the dusk, crickets begin their serenade,
and neighbors whack down green things in their yards
that are apparently growing too much –

greenery that is in fact a gift from the gods –
life and lushness spilling over the edges –
and here we are, straining every hour
to contain it.

Part IV

Half a Century In

my face feels worn –
every pockmark tells a story.

Suddenly,
things happened fifteen years ago,
like the Old Man of the Mountain,
falling.

Lost Thoughts

Every day, words are being erased –
I don't know what replaces them.

Hard to think
I was intelligent, once,
as I scramble for words now –
names of things, of people –
my lost thoughts trail in eddies
and get tangled in thickets.

Lost thoughts
blanket the mind like falling snow.
Where oh where did the brain cells
that made me
go?

Summer Library

In the library, too, we are tired –
we have melted into the furniture,
and are snoring softly,
we older folk
who came in for respite from the searing heat.

Drought-ridden trees wave silently,
as if beseeching us
in the courtyard, behind the glass,
shaming us for this ungodly heat.

It suddenly feels epic, here in the library –
a monumental miasma of global warming
and intellectual inertia and bodily rigor mortis,
as we slip into yet another unquenchable nap.

Dust Bowl on TV

Look what you did,
fools!

You ripped up my protective coat –
15 inches of Buffalo grass –
and killed all the buffalo, too,
while you were at it.
You left my bare body exposed
to the wind and drought
which blew it away.

You killed the coyote
that kept the jack rabbits in check,
and then you killed them too, with sticks,
when, famished,
they ate the only green things left.

You killed your own cattle
when all you had to feed them was tumbleweed.
And then came the grasshopper plague
which you treated with poison, of course

and then the dead and dying children –
truly, it was biblical.

Proving once again
that every little thing
affects every single thing,
and you can truly count on humans
to destroy that chain,
over and over again.

I Can See Why Sylvia Plath Killed Herself

This world is just too much sometimes,
with its Holocausts and factory farms,
too awful to bear –
with its slaughtered elephants
and spilled intestines, everywhere.

We wear tattoos, all of us
on our backs and bodies –
the scar tissue of childhood slights
and every stupid thing
we ever did or said.

The brutal cold of winter
Does. Not. Help.
nor the crying of children,
when all each of us ever wants
is love and birds and springtime.

A Prayer for Rough Sleepers

Someone, give us the strength
to survive this particular onslaught
of cell-death and other indignities,

to live through this special riot
of political mayhem and refugee-making,
this nonstop deforestation and sickening life-taking.

Help us find a way to praise the magic
of returning birds in springtime,
of hurt cells finally healing,
and of rough sleepers everywhere
soothed and cradled, loved and placated,
asleep in the right kind of arms.

Kindred Spirits

I want you to enjoy
the vicissitudes of existence,
my dear friends –

I wish you to be cosseted
by so many things of beauty –
to taste this delicate tea,
to read this astounding novel,
to be dazzled by these fall-blooming flowers.

Your singular souls, your beings,
are a blessing to me –
like they were to Rumi,

and as big as all the great stories
in the world.

Grateful for Parties

My husband fixed
the broken plates after the party,
and the shredded antique magazine
I'd stupidly put on display,

though we had to throw away
the broken chair that fell to pieces
under the overly-exuberant house guest,
and we could not fix the exhaustion
engendered by throwing parties
in your own tender home.

But we love our dear friends,
really we do!
and their drunken boyfriends and neighbors, too!
What do we have in this world,
if not our friends?

Only time
makes you grateful
for parties.

Making the Stew

It's a gift,
this lentil soup –
latterly slender orange discs in a glass jar,
to which I add water and spices
and boil, stirring,
for quite some time.

It's a gift,
from me to you,
humble husband who does not cook –
my rare bit of kitchen alchemy
and seeming magic.
I stir in cumin, coriander and turmeric,
tomato paste and a bay leaf,
and add whatever veggies
still eke out a living in the crisper.

And then lo!
An hour and a half later,
It all magically coalesces into our evening meal –
one I serve casually,
although it is, in fact,

quite a feat and gift from the planet,
and just in time for our show,
"The Durrells in Corfu."

These Limpid Days

Are the best, in my book –
everything growing green
and hanging low, giddy with being.

Sure, the basement reeks,
but it's the weekend
and I'm on a chair on the sun porch,
watching the sunset and reading poems,

having walked the dogs
and talked with the neighbors
and decided that I love them all,
Whitman-esque, to the core of their very beings –

our fallible bodies,
how we talk about everything and nothing –

and how ridiculously grateful I am now
for whatever divine forces brought me here,
to this very porch, this very summertime.

Hosta Horns

The throbbing heart tells itself
 despite all difficulties
"only connect!"

It cannot stop pumping,
so open the windows
and let the green world in,
hosta horns unfurling.

Revel in the yellow-leafed sunshine
and let the joyful morning dog lick your face.

For Layla

Nicknames for my dog include:
Little Bear
Honey Wags
and Silence Von Gruff.

Really, she doesn't ask for much –
just to follow you from room to room
with shiny eyes
full of love.

Acknowledgements

I would like to thank my husband Rich and my friends over the years for their support and encouragement, especially "The Poetry Sisters," and my fabulous Facebook friends far and wide.

I'd also like to thank the editors in which the following poems first appeared:

Nixes Mate Review: "An American Girl" and "Bait Dogs"
Writing in a Woman's Voice: "Blue Blanket," "Kind Women" and "Springing"
The Lily Review: "Babies in Jam Jars"
The Mayor's Office of Arts & Culture, Boston: "Green Gift"

About the Author

Karen Friedland, a grant writer by trade, lives in a quiet neighborhood on the edge of Boston with her husband, two cats and two dogs. Her work has been published in *Nixes Mate Review, Writing in a Woman's Voice, Sojourner* newspaper and others. She is the interviewer for Červená Barva Press, and is a founding member of the Poetry Sisters collective. She is proud to have recently had a poem selected by the Boston Poet Laureate to be displayed for 12 months at Boston City Hall.

42° 19′ 47.9″ N   70° 56′ 43.9″ W

Nixes Mate is a navigational hazard in Boston Harbor used during the colonial period to gibbet and hang pirates and mutineers.

Nixes Mate Books features small-batch artisanal literature, created by writers who use all 26 letters of the alphabet and then some, honing their craft the time-honored way: one line at a time.

nixesmate.pub/books

www.ingramcontent.com/pod-product-compliance
Lightning Source LLC
Chambersburg PA
CBHW052105110526
44591CB00013B/2363